Rants and Raves

Selected and New Prose Poems
Peter Johnson

White Pine Press, Buffalo, New York 14201

Acknowledgments

Pretty Happy! (1997), *Miracles & Mortifications* (2001), and *Eduardo & "I"* (2006) were first published by White Pine Press. Dennis Maloney, Editor.

Poems from the "Travels with Gigi" section of *Miracles & Mortifications* were first published as *Love Poems for the Millennium* (1998) by Quale Press. Gian Lombardo, Editor.

Thanks to Steve Frech and Oneiros Press for reproducing "American Male, Acting Up" as a broadside.

Grateful acknowledgment is made to the editors of the following magazines in which some of these poems or versions thereof first appeared:

The Alembic, The American Poetry Review, Another Chicago Magazine, Asylum Annual, Barnabe Mountain Review, Boulevard, Bryant Literary Review, Caesura, Caprice, Chiron Review, Clock Radio, Colorado Review, Del Sol Review, Denver Quarterly, Dislocate, DMQ, Double Room, 88, Epoch, Field, 5 a.m., Five Fingers Review, Green Mountains Review, Indiana Review, In Posse Review, The Iowa Review, key satch(el), Luna, The Mickle Street Review, Mind in Motion, Mississippi Review, New American Writing, North Dakota Quarterly, Panoply, Pig Iron, Ploughshares, Poetry East, The Potomac, Quarterly West, Sentence, Silverfish Review, Soundings East, Tendril, Third Coast, TriQuarterly, Untitled, Verse, The Wormwood Review, and *Yet Another Small Magazine.*

Continued on page 105

Published by: White Pine Press
P.O. Box 236
Buffalo, New York 14201
www.whitepine.org

Book and cover design by R. Newell Elkington.

First Edition.

ISBN 978-1-935210-06-1

Printed and bound in the United States of America

Library of Congress Control Number: 2009937820

for Genevieve, Kurt, Lucas, and especially Jeanne

Adios Amigos

—The Ramones (1995)

Table of Contents

Pretty Happy! (1997)

Miracles & Mortifications (2001)

"Travels with Gigi"

Eduardo & "I" (2006)

Table of Contents *continued*

New Poems

Pretty Happy!

I have no siblings who've killed themselves, a few break-downs here and there, my son sometimes talking back to me, but, in general, I'm pretty happy. And if the basement leaks, and fuses fart out when the coffee machine comes on, and if the pastor beats us up with the same old parables, and raccoons overturn the garbage cans and ham it up at two o'clock in the morning while some punk is cutting the wires on my car stereo, I can still say, I'm pretty happy.

Pretty happy! Pretty happy! I whisper to my wife at mid-night, waking to another night noise, reaching for the baseball bat I keep hidden under our bed.

Nettles

"She was running in the field with the tall nettles," but there were no nettles in my neighborhood. Just a line I stole. But she was running in the field. There was a fight, and I looked on in tranquil wonder. Chains, like bats, flying from black leather jackets. She was yelling, "Get help," knives swaying back and forth in the tall field. I yanked on my scapular. She was running because it was over her, because of things she did I could only imagine. She was running, barefoot and bruised in the tall field. She had never heard the word "nettles." Even I wouldn't come upon it until years later.

Penates

My father is omniscient. He says, "When I'm right, I'm right, and when I'm wrong, I'm right." So he's infallible, too. High above us, he rides his crane, his large, white eye illuminating our bedroom window, or he slides under the door on the blue vapor of the TV. For lunch, peanut butter, or the tang of ore dust on outstretched tongues—rats killed by pouring jagged pieces of glass around the foundation. "Seal their holes with concrete blocks," my father says. At twilight, we burrow beneath the swing set. Mother should say, "Wait until your father comes home," but instead, "If you dig a hole, you'll have to bury someone in it." Behind her, father's sad eye blinks.

Easter, Circa 1960

Such a clattering of black shoes. Mine are very tight and have pointed toes. "Spic shoes," my grandfather calls them, which is fine with me, as I fashion my pompadour and place a gangster-style hat on my head. My cheeks are fat, my pants tight around my ass. A boy was stabbed yesterday. I stood with the older boys and watched—the arc of the knife's blade like a silver fish rising for water spiders. The kitchen table glows with bowls of shrimp and hot cocktail sauce. A giant urn of potato chips gives shape to the living room. After dinner, my father argues with my grandparents, and everyone goes home. I take the chips to my room. Lie down. Click my Cuban heels.

Moses

I believe in the God of the Hebrews and also Moses, but know them only through movies. "Moses, Moses," on Pharaoh's dying lips. I think of Moses, impressed by his durability. The first sight of unending sand would have driven me down. I'd have been all over Jethro's daughters like a hot Israeli robe.... An old theater, large, golden snakes writhing on the circular ceiling, imitation gargoyles on brass balcony railings, seats so soft they could swallow you up. On screen, Moses and his long, gray hair, Moses parting the Red Sea, Moses on our lips at Nick's where you could buy four red-hots for a dollar. At the bus stop not even Moses able to keep four kids from pummeling an old lady with her own purse. A black leather purse, with two fake diamonds flashing under the streetlights.

Testimony

Today I learned "gomez" meant ox urine. It was a day fat with the flight of errant soccer balls, my son refusing for the first time to hold my hand. I wanted to tell my wife about that, but all I could say was "floating" and "prison." I wanted a chauffeur. I wanted to pick up the chauffeur-phone and say, "James, please bring up the car. I have a soccer game to attend." At night, the stars on my son's ceiling anchor the room. "Stars." "Room." I hold his limp hand and whisper, "floating," "prison." With my thumb, I draw soft lines on my wife's face, rest my head on her lap. In the kitchen, the cat's playing with his food, ice cubes hardening at the mere thought of "drink."

Guy Talk

My son asks, "What does it mean when you're watching TV and your dick gets hard?" "Change the channel," I say, "and when you speak to me, call your dick a penis." Though I never did. We had more names for our penises than the Greeks had for gods: pecker, dink, swanzola.... You've heard them, seen the boys laughing behind the sand dunes lost in their fathers' dirty magazines. What fascination! How they simultaneously run and grip themselves while filling the air with soccer balls. How, as adults, these same boys display and measure their members on a specially designed cutting board, so that afterwards, a pecker order decided, they can speak honestly with each other. If just for a moment.

Open House

It's not easy to love oneself. Just yesterday, no one would speak to me at the open house. So many parents, I wanted to write them letters, or share my pineapple squares. But they were camped out by the salad bar, so far away it was like a dream, except for the heartburn. Even the hot dogs looked sad, tugged this way and that between two stainless steel rollers. I ate one. My son had pizza. Then I sat in his classroom, scanning a history book, hoping a different time period might present itself. I raised my hand to pee, but the teacher punished me with dirty looks. "I was president of the fourth grade," I protested, "chosen to crown the Virgin on May Day." The children scowled, threatening me with their No. 2 pencils. Even the portrait of Cortez seemed angry as I traced his bloody March across Mexico.

Scavengers!

My birdfeeder, pagoda of weathered wood, its floor scattered with dry seeds and corn that glitter in the sunlight like pieces of gold. It rests atop a pole I sledgehammered into the ground, with hopes for a cardinal, maybe even an oriole. But not a pigeon, certainly not four, their asses hanging from the rim. Pigeons, gluttonous, like rats; like cows shitting everywhere. I scatter them with a hard spray, the one I save for hub-caps, for scouring the driveway. Their wings flap manic, like damp sheets caught in the wind. A kind of hazing, I know. And for whose benefit? The good birds? Pretty birds? Melodious warblers? All winter I feed and photograph them, and then the spring arrives, nuts and berries everywhere, every imaginable seedling—I just a silhouette, spying from an upstairs window. A laughingstock: old daddy-longlegs clinging to the minute hand of our rusty, outdoor clock; the anemic worm stranded on a slab of concrete, the hot, August sun just now on the rise.

Lover Boys

I saw the movie where Indiana Jones and his father make love to the same beautiful German spy, and I wondered if my father and I could do that. Of course, she wouldn't be a German spy. Probably just some big-hearted, fat-lipped donut girl with no self-respect. Or maybe just someone who was terribly lonely. She'd suffer, that's for sure: in cheap Italian restaurants with my father, munching suspect meatballs and fish 'n' chips; or with me, forced to confess every wet detail of the night the high school quarterback lapped maple syrup from her navel. Until that one inevitable morning when she'd scan the legal section of the Yellow Pages, or maybe just give up and leap off a bridge.

An absurd scenario? Perhaps. For one thing, my father and I don't live in the same city anymore, and when we did, we couldn't even share the La-Z-Boy without fighting.

Sibling Rivalry

I have no older sister, so I'm surprised when she shows up at my birthday party. A gorgeous creature, my sister, despite the tiny tattoo of a spider twitching on her forehead as she toothpicks tabouli from her teeth. She's here to say I got the genes for cancer and premature gray hair. A real study in undifferentiated anger, my sister. "Live simply so others may simply live," she hisses, then heads for the potato chips. Easy for her to say. She was father's favorite, slept in a pink canopied bed next to a large drinking dish reserved for endangered species. The kind of sister who could have changed my life, but she doesn't show up until now, her Little Miss Western Civilization banner draped across her breasts. That's just like my sister, the one I never had, the one I can't remember.

The Genius

Look out Flaubert! Move over Joyce! He slept on a mattress stuffed with old first editions and women's shoes. Stayed up late, this Genius, touching himself, anticipating nocturnal omissions. He strung brilliant sounds together—"mustang bang," "laughable liaisons"—and built a portable pedestal he dragged from city to city, reading his poetry and romancing Rubenesque librarians. "Sonny, oh, Sonny," they'd say, "you're a Genius." One rainy day, he retrieved an orange prescription bottle floating toward a sewer. In it this note: "Immediately, if not sooner." A judgment? A prognostication? That's the trouble with Genius, it's so very hard to pin down.

Hell

"If you want to understand the social and political history of modern man, study hell."
— *Thomas Merton*

It's probably like the excitement of your first cigarette, but it lasts forever, that dizzying nausea—the Unknown: sulphuric clouds, infernal helpers scurrying around with imitation human heads on their buttocks, bats leaping from black books, dragon tails waving, monkey glands everywhere, hope dying slowly like a bad marriage, "I am nobody" the only conversation. But then again the damned might be as recognizable and stupid as the living: men who use the same condom twice, women who let them, the degenerate who molested Spider-Man—everyone perpetually suing each other, holding hands in a circle whose rim clangs like a counterfeit coin. But more likely it's the general humiliation of being dead, realizing your own personal Beelzebub might be the least weird guy you know.

The Provider

Let's say you're at the company Christmas party and the boss orders everyone to unscrew their heads and drop them into a large bamboo basket. Now what should you do when you're the last one to choose a head, and the one left isn't yours, and you can feel it isn't yours, even though everyone swears they have the right heads on, and your boss gets angry and says, "Of course that's your head, and if you want to keep your job, you better screw it on tightly"?

Or let's say on a Sunday morning you and your family leave home for a picnic. Now we're talking about your split-level home you've worked so hard for, with its manicured lawn and electric garage door, located in the best school district in the city.

Now what should you do if while you and your family are barbecuing, black hooded figures break into your home, pulverize its contents with sledgehammers, empty the pieces into large, green, plastic garbage bags, which they stack along your front sidewalk, then level the house by detonating sticks of dynamite planted in the baby's bedroom?

I, for one, seriously consider these questions, which is why I never hold a steady job, and why I frequently move my family, making sure they have no place to call home.

19th-Hole Condom Poem

Failed poet completes "19th-Hole Condom Poem," about a light green condom with a little flag on top. For it to work, its wearer must yell "Fore" when he climaxes.

The poem is published and praised by a group of editors interested in poetry, golf, and kinky sex. It's chosen as one of the best poems of the year. To one critic, the poem is "an attack on the sensibility of the idle rich"; to another, a metaphor for the "failure of the American imagination, the symbol of the 19th Hole equal in resonance to Melville's white whale."

The poet's luck changes; all his work is accepted. No longer do poems come back wrinkled or with coffee stains. No longer do editors write, "This isn't poetry, it's truth," or, "We're not into nature, we publish only working-class poems."

He's even offered a full professorship at a major university where he hardly teaches and is surrounded by women in black linen dresses who write poems to their dead fathers. He makes friends with other poets and reads his poetry for $1000 a shot. He's frequently interviewed, asked what sock he puts on first in the morning.

He enjoys all this tremendously until he's unable to write. He gets fat, develops prostate problems, and talks too much. But he has tenure, a year's membership in the golf club, and new students keep arriving in search of the author of the famous "19th-Hole Condom Poem."

The Millennium

In the basement, in the playroom, Ken's throwing darts at another Ken while the flies of fairy tales nod off on a concrete wall, on a red plunger by the sink, on a lonesome cue ball. Upstairs, a pair of twins dancing on a hardwood floor, pushing tiny Santas in miniature baby strollers. I need help to sit down. "Next you'll be wanting a back rub," my brother says, then leaps from a coffee table, toppling our Christmas tree. Not enough bulbs to poke holes through this night's black logic. No one strong enough to turn The Great Telescope, still partially unwrapped.

Four hours to midnight, my niece embracing her Sleepy-Time Barbie, eyelids set to close at the turn of the century.

Home

Nighttime. I'm hitched to a machine, nursing a noun, tapping a verb on its shoulder, apposing appositives. Moments earlier, I was cruising the Internet, taping, then dancing to, national anthems of my favorite countries. "We never go anywhere," I complained, maneuvering colored tacks around my wall-sized atlas. My vertebra had cracked; that's what happened. Then it healed, now just an incredible longing for travel. This morning, tiny children hung upside down from damp branches of our dogwood tree, whispering *baby, baby, baby.* A premonition? A warning? Sure feels like a baby's brewing, someone to keep company with our tow-headed boy asleep in his prince-sized bed. Burnt popcorn! Pigeons shitting on the patio! Insatiability of tomato worms! This is "home." But also our Treasure Island bedsheets, with an ancient map of someone's tropical paradise. It looks like a board game. "Gigi, I beg you to come closer." And your response? "Don't call me that." It's a childhood nickname, but one that stuck . . . Bedtime, all bashfulness banished. Quiet, save the croaking of a few insomniac crickets and the roar of a Harley. Tonight we'll tumble down Love's dark hole, a trail of responsibilities, like breadcrumbs, behind us. "Set the bed for vibrate," I whisper, wondering who'll make the first move.

Paris

A white poodle named Gigi. A fingernail red as the fire breather's face, red as my sparrow's neck, which you sometimes touch. Louis XIV boasted, "I am the State." Rimbaud, "Je est un autre." But I respond, "Je ne comprend pas." To come so far and stumble over a poodle named Gigi beneath an ancient fountain, beneath a tarnished Greek statue— his beard of seaweed, his baton and chiseled smirk. Impossible to be so sad beside this school of oversized goldfish and a poodle named Gigi. "Dear fated name!" So accustomed to miracles was Abelard, yet humbled by the pale of Eloisa's shoulders, her oval mouth, as I am also. How my Gigi-magician pulls silk panties from our hotel dresser, like colored tissues from a fancy box. How she mocks my cotton pajamas until I yell in protest, "Forehead" or "Foreskin."

This white poodle named Gigi, by a fountain, begging for a bone.
To whom shall I give it?

Costa Rica

Whatever Gigi wants, Gigi gets. This time it's the day-flying, cyanide-filled moth, *Urania ripheus*, infamous for copulating with different species. "Ugh! Yuk! There's a bug, squash it," I tease, not wanting to burst from my hammock-cocoon. I wanted to help but had promised our host, René, that I'd clean the poison frog garden. Then I remembered this aphorism: "Universal hostility and fear toward a species are the products of ignorance." I also remembered Gigi's promise of a juicy love-bite to be given beneath a huge banana tree near the forking paths . . . Long-curved leaves the size of scimitars, bright green spikes of plantains, and a white-skinned woman, her bare breasts barely the size of serpent eggs, her dark eyebrows alert, like two facing centipedes. I'm adjusting my loincloth, then waving my butterfly net made from a clothes hanger and the thinnest of Gigi's panties. "Leaping lepidoptera. I got one." Two ear-sized wings fringed with golden hair, its underside red and veined like a tiny heart. Drip drop, drip drop. Then naked we lie beneath our banana tree, bold as two mottled stink bugs. I hold the moth between my fingers, then let go. "Erotic things occur in the rain," Gigi whispers, about to sink her teeth into my neck.

Provincetown

We laughed about the pine tree laying its eggs, the blue fright wig I bought last Halloween, then a little wine, and a little more. The bed next door began creaking a foreign, same-sex language. I was reading a thin book wherein a fat lady wrestles with nouns. A book taking sixty years to flower. Later, we stumbled into a tree-shaded courtyard where white marble lions drank from an albatross' basin. We had run out of booze, and I kept having to pee. "So go one last time," and "Okay, I will." The mean mosaic of the courtyard floor was making me dizzy, anyway. Off-season, the narrow streets were barren, the frigid, salt air from another century when wreckers scoured the beaches for boxes and barrels. "Gigi," I said, "in the fall the cows here often feed on cod's head! Did you know that?" "And capybaras have webbed feet and are excellent swimmers," she replied, understanding my foreplay. We would have continued if not for a large poster of a petrified, Amazonian face eyeballing us from a tarred telephone pole. "The Fat Bitch Is Back," the poster announced. And we had to believe it, suddenly confronted by a woman dressed like a bird cage, and another like an umbrella. Really nice people, though, in spite of their cheap costumes. "Are we hungry yet? Are we downright famished?" Gigi nodded, knowing a loss is not a great loss, and that the liquor stores didn't close until midnight.

Geneva

Banished from one writer's colony for blowing the whistle on a certain Southern plagiarist, this is true. Booed at The Great Poetry Slam, true again. Not to mention a certain liaison with a long-stemmed reference librarian who slashed Gigi with a letter opener for reading our love letters. This time, they promised we'd be "drunken, expatriate writers" for two weeks and that the roast beef sandwiches would be juicy. Just clean tables and look intelligent, write a few poems now and then. So I grew a handlebar moustache to mimic the horny social-activist poet who tried to skim the skin with Gigi while she served the sorbet. He had seen her play tennis and was, as he said, "overhauled by her overhand." I continued to clean the antique wooden tables of lettuce scraps and garbanzo beans, thinking of a good place to hide Gigi's racket. Fortunately, we were saved by a telegram announcing that I had won "The-Man-Least-In-Touch-With-His-Feminine-Side Contest." A strange contest indeed, especially since I didn't enter it. And the reward? Fifty dollars and two weeks in Geneva to study with the author of the trilogy *He, She,* and *It*—a man steeped in *paternalia* who enigmatically fingered his fly, asking over and over, "Who are you really, La-La Boy?" In a dimly lit room, he tightened leather straps around my wrists, tied a rooster to my desk and ordered it to peck out my eyes. But the rooster was really a French poet who'd been transformed into a rooster for sticking pins into chickens for the fun of it. The rooster-poet balked. "Who are you really?" my tormentor demanded, his white head looking as if it had been fetched from a freezer, his almond-shaped hands quivering. *Je suis Gigi,* is what came to me, and "Je suis Gigi," is what I said. As if on cue, her ancient, wooden racket came crashing through my blackened window, signifying both triumph and rescue . . . Later, a stiff wind off Lake Geneva, Gigi stroking my hair, feeding me tiny chocolates stolen from a local confectionary. I'm staring into a white, head-shaped cloud, my universe running in reverse, my own head haunted by the vision of a half-stitched Frankenstein, searching the mountainside for his father. An odd thought, if not for the insight of our rooster-poet, who keeps reciting in impeccable French: "Even the dumbest dreams astound us."

Fiesole

Intrigues are exhausting, so are pets and professors, photographers and poets. It's a long walk to the orange groves, especially when I was ordered to stay home. This time, Gigi clothed in little besides a fishnet tank top and a pair of sky-blue running shoes. Brand new shoes, the gel still ungelled. Shoes attached to her ankles, her ankles to her calves, her calves to her thighs—parts poeticized by this skinny Polish photographer in black, skin-tight Levis who could pass for a child, except for the scar across his forehead and missing left thumb. Cowering behind a mossy boulder, I look and listen: "A little kick this time," he laughs, and Gigi complies, awakening a squadron of fruit flies. It's early, still damp, the dew frozen on branches and orange blossoms, which look like fancy glass-blown earrings. Now he tells her to shed her tank top, and I think, *It's time to leave for Rome*. Yes! I have the urge to go Roman, to order broad-shouldered, Amazonian slaves to lug ice from nearby mountains and blend it with honey and fruit juices. Then I'll behead them. But we're not in Rome; just a cloud of fruit flies, and Gigi, bare-naked in her sky-blue running shoes. I swear it!

Greenland

Icebergs the size of great ships melting in a blue fiord; large stones un-
disturbed for centuries; white-haired grandmothers in a hot spring, their
heads bobbing like the flared nostrils of hippopotami a thousand miles
away. Permanence. Eskimo strength, suckled by the blood of Eric the
Red. You hear that, Gigi? Permanence. Predictability—like the small, stoic
potatoes this cold earth gives up. Tough, like these grandmothers who
won't leave earth when they die; instead expire on arctic boulders, where
caught by moonlight, they flap like a catch of capelin. In the morning, just
a pack of seals breathing heavily in a shine of water as black as love. And
why are we here? Everyone together: Because in Notre Dame, Gigi made
a pass at her wrist with a razor and called me her "quasi-Quasimodo,"
displaying a cracked picture to prove it. I blamed it on a little French girl's
behind and two fish swimming in opposite directions . . . I'm on my way to
her cabin, carrying a bottle of Australian wine and a bag of Cheetos, my
boots battling a moat of tundra vegetation. Gigi's in a lamp-lit window,
pounding brown dough into phallic shapes, then massaging them with
a cube of white butter. "Now sleeps the crimson petal, now the white," I
sigh, which somehow consoles me. And also the fact that Greenland has
no trees. Nowhere for an anxious lover to hang himself. No trees, few
vegetables, just rocks. Permanence. Stick-to-itiveness. So I leave, drag-
ging my long tale of sins behind me. Later I cover myself with seal skins
and read aloud in my canvas cot. It's a little book of love poems, one
box-shaped, like a window, through which a sandy coast appears, tall
cypresses swaying like showgirls, beckoning.

On Bastille Day in Notre Dame, Gigi parted her thickly painted lips
and whispered to an astonished art historian, "I love to watch naked
men play."

I tell you, comments like that drive me crazy.

Palm Springs

Maxing out stolen credit cards, we know a week from now they'll never find us. We're out to prove Love has no landlord—that is, you can't hit a moving target. But how to reckon these peculiarities: a fat, black spider dangling from our obligatory fake chandelier; the soft, caterpillar moustache of our blondie-boy pool attendant; and a pack of paparazzi downing shots as two Mexicans are clubbed senseless on TV. Now this is American history! Gigi's fashioning her toothbrush into a skeleton key. I'm hardening my belly to look like the baroque bread board I spied in the souvenir shop. Later, I loiter around the porcelain dog bar with a bow-tied poodle dressed like a Vanderbilt, his owner's herringbone, golden necklace awash on her breast. Try to be friendly, I think, and so offer to interpret her surgical chart—her face-lifts, tummy tucks. "You'd make a good pet," she purrs, blaming her flirtation on a gene she inherited for ass-biting, passed down from one anxious countess to another. If I just had my golf clubs, I'd stay here forever. What a place, where women come dripping out of pools, slick as seals, their empty eye sockets bathed in sunlight, their calf muscles hardening like pears. I could get rejuveniled here. But don't tell Gigi, who's just returned with the loot and a bottle of imported Scotch . . . A little ice, some natural darkness, and a moon frozen in the sky like a pale Frisbee thrown by the hand of God. I tell her, "Receiving a stolen gift is naughty but erotic," then accept the pen she gives me with its skin of hardest opal. Tonight a team of cosmonauts passes quietly overhead. In the morning, we try to break from each other's grip, but the bedroom mirror hardens us.

Barcelona

Moonlight softens the hardwood floor. A wind-blown, hundred-year-old dust ball scurries under the bed. And a fat black spider—our love child—awakens; its legs bloom, its web shimmers, like lace panties stretched tightly and held up to the sun. We are resting after a day of massaging my moods. "Happy love has no history," I whisper. But tonight that's hard to believe. Annoyed by the chi-chi shops and capitalists speaking Catalonian into their cellular phones, we went to the cathedral to view St. Eulalia's crypt. It was very quiet, and I said I couldn't remember anything until the age of forty-one when I saw you step out of an elevator. Perhaps that's why you are so quiet tonight, naked except for a collar of Majorcan pearls. "If you come to Barcelona," I would tell tourists, "you will see this and you will discover that, and you will find my Gigi kneeling before the crypt of St. Eulalia. And you will think, *Someone should tell their stories; someone should tell them they are beautiful.*"

Tex-Mex

"Everything in this world passes, but Love will last forever." If this is true, then where is my Gigi this morning? I am naked, half-embalmed, like a worm at the bottom of a brown bottle, a certain black-eyed Susan curled around my leg, only the sound of my palomino weeping in the prairie grass. My battery is dead, my cactus has growing pains . . . We were searching for the Old Dutchman's mine, our guide Buck a consummate rough rider in every kind of saddle. Joe the Bad and Jim the Ugly brought up the rear. "Call me Blue or Coyote," I drawled, which made Gigi laugh. Or was it my Styrofoam pith helmet with the smiley-face decal on front? "We'll be breaking virgin territory," Buck grunted, but all I saw was a huge pyramid of cast-off microwave ovens. The day wore on, the sun dragging it westward like a withered foot. We shot a few elk and wild pigs, milked some rattlesnakes. At the hoedown at Apache Jack's, we shared campfire stories. "I had a cheesy childhood," I began, "one with many holes in it, and a heavy Thing, a Thing like the last tree left standing so you can build a house around it." "When you're done, Stretch," Buck said, opening a large, brown bottle of mescal, "can you pass the beans?" And what do I remember? The raw outline of a covered wagon branded on Buck's forearm, his red hair bristling like porcupine quills, then bushwhacked I was by a certain black-eyed Susan, whose snoring now seems as cruel as hunger—the price to pay for going home with the wrong Gigi.

Cannes

A poached egg without the pocket, embarrassed before the tongue's eye. Have you ever felt like that? Cagey croissant bars, two baby shrimp cavorting on a bed of artichokes, floating houses, flying fish, and sleek limousines squatting in front of Belle Epoch hotels—a splendid cubist landscape, yet here we are encamped on a beach in moth-eaten sleeping bags. In this take, Gigi's a nun. Not *like* a nun, but a real one—at least in her mind. "Nun, the feminine of *nonnus*—old man." We're talking bodily integrity! Virginity! What a laugh. I was up early, sucking on my kava kava Think! Bar, drawing a huge smiley face on our hotel ceiling with a piece of lipstick tied to the tip of a bamboo pole. Then I decided to buy a newspaper. Came back to a certain Gigi sitting upright in bed, wearing her plum edible panties and a white T-shirt emblazoned with the image of Sean Penn. She was aglow, people, that's a fact. Later she explained:

> He appeared on the red wallpaper! My flesh fell to the floor.
> I was stripped by lightning! ... What beauty! What elegance
> and sweetness! His shoulders, his bearing! Such a peaceful
> shining face!

Who was I to doubt, though there was something familiar about this ecstasy. And it came to pass ... Gigi and I giving alms, warning the infidels to heal themselves, making pilgrimages to the cell of The Man in the Iron Mask—all the time my orchids swelling beneath my cassock, unable to look away from the near espresso tans of half-naked starlets and hangers-on. "According to *A New Catholic Dictionary*," I warned, "ecstasies as a rule do not last long." But she'd have none of it. And my last image of these days? Waking on the beach, a morning sea breeze toying with Sister Gigi's white cotton robe, her Holiness rolling onto her side exposing a pale cheek. A miracle? An optical illusion? No, just a tattoo of winged old St. Michael, waving his shiny, righteous sword in my face, his long blond, Nordic locks flaming behind him.

Sydney

The universe expands, we feel its pull, its tug . . . The day awakens, brimming with brawn. We're crooked, my Gigi-girl and me, that is, slipped from our moorings. I mean, hungover. Consider last night's adventure at the Wombat Bar and Grill, our Captain balancing a tinny of beer on his bare belly, farting like a Piper Cub. Was this the great shark hunter? The man who rode six hundred pound turtles? Who broke a swamp fever by clinging to the body of a dead buffalo? Who kept a collection of exotic monkeys in his cellar? "Bunga, bunga, who's got the bunga," Gigi laughs, showing a bit of thigh through her straw skirt. "For an ordinary couple to have extraordinary sex," is what she really wanted—thus a tooth extracted from a great white shark captured at dusk, "then pulverized," she said, "stirred in a glass of tepid kiwi juice." I wanted a damp terry-cloth towel to wrap around my aching head, but, as it was written, "The day awakens, brimming with brawn. . . ." Three mates on board, all with identical blond moustaches, as if hatched from the same pouch. The Captain's donning his sharkskin hat, and, at long last, a glimpse of his famous webbed feet. "G'day," he says, squinting toward the horizon through a pair of leathery eyelids. "G'day, bonza," we reply. What can I say, mates? A long day, the ocean turning blood-red for the sake of love, and then our return—the Captain's small craft knocking on the harbor's dimwitted door, a fog horn weeping like a hero. And let's not forget that blood-stained shark's tooth buried deep in a damp pocket of Gigi's bra—as beautiful and absurd as any glass slipper.

Night, New York all gussied up. So much to do, but we're afraid to go out. Calf brains, hair from a wolf's tail, snake bone, even bits of a human corpse—ritually laid out on our bed. Love potions, uncocked concoctions to ward off suitors. We're waiting for a giant ape. "Do I look boxy?" Gigi asks, eyeing her hips in the bedroom mirror. She's fashioning an ape-like man from sugar cubes, setting a pitcher of warm tea next to him. So why are we afraid? Has the young master lost his wits? It was my fault. Sick of puzzling over the lines on my palms, sick of diving into holy lakes, I went to find the tribe who invented zero. I mean, I was searching for The Secret. But we got lost in the jungle, then captured by hard-bellied, coffee-colored virgins, who smeared my body with resin and blew gold dust on me until I glistened from head to toe. Unfortunately, they were hitched to a giant ape, who himself fell hard for Gigi. He tried to hold her gently like a small banana but bruised her egg-white thighs. "Unhand her," I yelled, reminding him of a basic, irrefutable Rule of Love: "Whatever nature forbids, Love is ashamed to accept." The last time we saw him he was wearing a giant, silly wreath of orchids around his head, trying to swat rescue helicopters. "He smelled worse than that vampire," Gigi says, dropping the sugar ape into the pitcher and watching him dissolve. Outside, small aircraft hover, then the rat-a-tat-tat of a machine gun, and a hairy digit of flesh fingering our hotel window. "Do you think he's come for my binoculars?" I laugh, diving into the love potions and rolling onto my back like a puppy.

Next day, standing near a giant tabernacle of ashes, the ape's weepy tribal princess speaks to the press. "I would have taken him back with no arms or legs," she says, "even if he were a stump."

Home

If there is no Gigi, there is still her name . . . To be sure, a long win-
ter, but now a spring breeze, like a sigh, carries us to the edge of our
sheets. Across the hall, a tow-headed boy moans, tumbling from one
clumsy dream to another. Adolescence—rascality, pure rascality! Tem-
pestuated, like the crocuses gazing up in a panic, all too aware of their
short-term erections. They know a Big Idea is ajar, our trip tripped. It
was all too exhausting, anyway—the hotels, the intrigues. Better to hun-
ker down, mine the backyard mulch for anemic worms, go fishing. Or
maybe lie still a moment, contemplate the scars on your feet, the ant-
sized beauty mark on your bum. The mailman sighs when you open the
front door in a silk kimono, I sigh when you open any door. I swear this
before our sharp-beaked lovebirds just now awakening in their golden
cage, exchanging necklaces crafted from the legs of a spider; before the
sacred shield of Jean de Jean, hanging in our garage next to the bicycle
rack; before my yang, growing warm, hard, steadfast. "See?" you laugh.
"This is how you get into trouble." And, of course, you're right. But our
fairy tale is fading—friends coupling and uncoupling in various unseem-
ly ways. So again I plead, "Speak louder to me, mother dear. A bit of
pancake, please, I am so hungry," and you pat me on the head and reply,
"Oh, darling, pretty, good, nice, clever, sweet darling . . ."

Departure

A new year! Yet no jubilation. Just a need to invent a language without coordination—as sinister as the history of a slave ship . . . I'm arranging my plaster-cast figures of famous men; you're leafing through *The Marquis de Sade's Everyday Collection.* Earlier, we fought over a cheap poster of a starlet's buttock. It was a cold afternoon, hard to think with all that yelling. "Make your bed!" "Take down that poster." "Don't put out cigarettes on the lovebirds!" "Do I ask too much?" I yell, then hurl a soiled Q-tip in your direction. I've heard confession helps: I confess to being a creature of detours, to stealing monogrammed towels from swank hotels. I even accept the savage history of my middle finger. But not you, O dearest boy, with a mind as tiny as Napoleon's hat, unforgiving as a nutcracker—Ouch! You, with your gelled head, slick and shiny as a seal's behind. Confess! Unburden yourself! And your teenangel response? "The true Daddy is against all Daddies." Later, huddling on your bed, we dive into the manic-depressed gene pool of the family photo album, our rescue team of women stranded in the soft snow outside. The poster's down, the starlet's tanned buttocks shivering on the hardwood floor. On the blank space of wall, a circular opening forms. An invitation? An escape? . . .

Socrates

Ah, the glory that was Greece! . . . excrement in the street and houses without windows. I wanted to teach you about Truth, which began as an idea rubbing its jaw against a rock, but ended up too tiny to shed its skin. *Gnothi seauton!* (Know Thyself!) What a laugh! "Good means intelligent." "Virtue means wisdom." And what of Socrates? The bugger had a booger in his nose the first time we saw him; still they followed him, happy as hoplites. He seduced you, too, with endless questions, scraps of reasoning. Then the Games—the agora looking like a homecoming weekend for dead philosophers, everyone talking in riddles. "Come home with your father," I said, and you answered, "What is father?" "Stop the nonsense," I ordered, and you asked, "What is its essential quality?" So I challenged Socrates to a wrestling match, but you took his place. Father and son. Mano a mano. What a testicular idea! . . . I'm leaning on a cypress, dressed in a loincloth, anointed with olive oil and dusted with white powder, my love handles and skinny legs a nightmare for any self-respecting bronze mirror. I'm led to a muddy pit, where you're squatting, all lathered and powdered like me. Lots of slapping, pushing, and sliding until I'm disqualified for face-biting. On my knees, blinded by a noonday sun, I'm barely able to spy Socrates as he approaches. "There's the story about a father," he laughs, "who swore he'd remain on earth as long as one son had need of him. Two days later, they found him hanging from an olive tree with an empty wine flask over his head."

Nero

Coins were struck, inscriptions inscribed, and monuments erected … *Ex gente Dimitiae duae familiae claruerunt*—I sing of Nero in a voice sweeter than that of Suetonius … Nero: wannabe poet and actor, haunted by the image of a poison mushroom the size of a Twinkie. Not exactly guilt, just too much inbreeding. "I dream of monkeys," he says. "I want to be buried with all my parts. I want to mount a woman concealed in the wooden image of Pasiphae. I want…." He's disgusting; if he smiles at you one more time, I'll castrate him, break his favorite enema bottle over his head, the one shaped like a Grecian urn. I came here looking for a natural cure for baldness; I wanted you to see a real vestal virgin. Instead, peasants rioting because of the price of bread, and this red-haired Romeo who couldn't even get a good grip on Agrippina. "The whole bunch of them are boring," you say, then make fart noises by cupping a hand under your armpit and flapping your elbow up and down. Astonished, the Emperor recoils, punctures his neck with an ornate, ceremonial knife. "Time to go," but first let's finish his uneaten feast: roast parrot and sweet sauce, boiled tree fungi, and sow udders stuffed with salted sea urchins—all washed down with hot African sweet-wine. And as for the Zippo lighter you smuggled through time? Leave it in the hot tub, something for future soothsayers and historians to consider.

Charlemagne

Who does not belong in this group: a. vassal; b. squire; c. scumsucking Saracen mounted on a pig? . . . Son, despite my sagging ass, the dithyrambic moaning of my spine, and my tongue's tantric rites, I've always wanted you to think me a Great Man. According to Sigmund, the Great Man exhibits traits of The Father. Let us ponder this remark, as we view the King Daddy of them all—his long white mane, thick and leathery neck. Corpulent, true, but strong and strong-willed, his broad chest protected by a jerkin made from the skins of otters and ermines. Both macho and Machiavellian but with the heartbeat of a little girl. He entered the world straddling the hump of a rainbow and, embarrassed by his comeliness, prayed nightly to be given the head of a rat. Was it he who said, "No beauty without deformity," in a tone as reasonable as the number one? "No, it was not he," you interrupt, "and the hump of the rainbow story is also nonsense." You're here, my varlet, both to jest and to joust. All night you lay awake listening to your pubic hair grow, fantasizing on veiled damsels, hot to unhorse Desiderata the Average, whose real name was Needlenose, just because he waved what he called his "enchanted lance" at the King's daughter. He arrives on horseback, accompanied by three Saracens—real angry guys with large black zeros on their backs, rusty chastity belts hanging from their saddles. "A real maiden cannot be made less," I offer in my Great Man voice, but you're not listening, your eyes flashing like an illuminated manuscript. Let the boys fight this one, let the squires squirm. I'm more interested in the golden hawk circling overhead with a pearl necklace dangling from its beak.

Monastic

I wanted self-discipline without the pain; you to catch a glimpse of a noon-day devil. Monk, from *monachus*, "someone who lives alone. . . ." We were working in the fields when a raven passed overhead, dropping a loaf of bread on us. In it an announcement of The Last Mortification Contest to be judged by the ghost of a hairy-chested fisherman. For one day, everyone would have the chance to be the Messiah. They paired us against a fat monk and his balding partner, who were famous for kissing stones, then lecturing them about responsibility. We began by eating little squares of bread sprin-kled with the ashes of nuns, then prostrating ourselves 666 times to create a sense of irony. For our finale, I displayed dried palm leaves wrapped around my back like a python. You soaked the leaves in camel's blood, scraping away the thorns with a scalpel fashioned from the claw of a peacock. Everyone cheered, even the pagan with a placard proclaiming: "Mendicants Masticate." A protest? A direct order? It was hard to tell. And the winners? Weighing in at a mere 110 lbs. each, direct from the devil-infested deserts of Egypt, two ancient anchorites who conjured up a pride of lions and convinced them to dig their own graves "forty baby fingers deep." It was the numerology that swayed the judge, who, amidst much psalm singing, presented the winners with a brand-new scourge and a bag of rock salt . . . Miracles and mortifica-tions, all of them, just to prove that sin is a habit!

Joan of Arc

... and there she sat with her breasts pressing against the tightly laced tunic, her fettered legs flung carelessly in front of her, the opening between her tunic and hose revealing the flesh of her thighs as far as the sketchy strip of linen that was no more than a *cache-sexe*.

Whoof! A dramatization, for sure, but one capturing your boyish imagination ... Jean la Pucelle! The Devil's Milkmaid! Armagnac Whore! Depends on your point of view. Just ask Cauchon, that crooked vessel of reason, only interested in who's getting The Treat. But we don't care about Cauchon. We've come for her thigh—not the white light streaming from her eyes, not the naked angel squatting on her left shoulder; not the chains on her neck and hands, nor the sacred bird nibbling squares of bread from her lap. Not even her scorched, holy heart, soon to be dragged along the bottom of the Seine. Let monks and historians chronicle these facts. It's her thigh we've come for, just a scrap of it— pearl-pale, creamy ... Oh, Lordy!

Johannes Kepler

I'm moored to my La-Z-Boy, a book of astronomy in hand, the rudder of my unheavenly ship broken (read "heart" for "rudder," blockheads). You're being punished for crushing my tinfoil replica of Mother Earth with a basketball. I hear you moving upstairs, dodging tiny glow-in-the-dark stars falling from your ceiling. You think my astronomical theories stink. Even the Big Questions bore you. To be honest, I'm just curious why my ass has dropped. Let's consult a wise man . . . Much not to like about Kepler. Tormented by classmates, smelling like a donkey, he's awaiting the music of the spheres. We come upon him beating Tycho Brahe with an ancient spy glass. "Be good to my bird," he chirps, trying to shake the celestial cacophony from his head. He's being held hostage by a circle, so you toss him a lovebird's elliptical egg, and . . . Eureka! Weeks later, passing out opiates, he warns of our imminent impact on the moon's surface. "Our bodies will roll themselves into balls," he says, "as spiders do, and we'll carry them by means of our will alone." Next thing, we're up to our ankles in moon dust, a star flaming by, borne on the back of a white dwarf. Kepler dons the mirrored, wraparound sunglasses you've brought him; I display a snapshot of Galileo's middle finger preserved in a marble and glass case. "It's like a baseball trophy," you explain, and he nods warily, dropping the sunglasses low onto his nose, breaking into a crazy dance as the Universe's Greatest Hits play on.

Samuel Johnson

The 18th century, thank God there's still a God—Order, Design, Right Reason not yet gone left. "You're *soooo* Johnsonian," my wife says, handing me a yellow pill. I'm obsessing again, tearing clumps of hair from my head, besieging the lovebirds with a dried-out drumstick. Depression—laughter and hypochondria create such strange cozenage. . . We're slopping our way to the Café Voltaire, pooped from last night's cockfight and boxing matches, beer and gin afflicting us in a dreadful manner. "I'll have no more on't," I keep yelling, not quite sure what I mean. At the fair you befriended an Irishman who shattered a chamber pot by barking Greek phrases from Sappho. Prostitutes mud-wrestling, fannies spanked with birch rods, then to the inoculation party where we drank cockroach tea while soaking our testicles in warm vinegar. "Not the lessons I wanted you to learn," I say, feeding a half-eaten tomato to a one-legged dog. Let me repeat: We're slopping our way to the Café Voltaire, sucking in coal dust, up to our ankles in uric mud, passing a ballad singer, an apple vendor, a dead horse. "By your leave," a fancy-pants personage apologizes, his black sedan nearly running me down. Later, I tell Johnson I'm homesick, but he offers this explanation: "Long intervals of pleasure dissipate attention and weaken constancy." And how right he is! "Wastrel, Johnny Boy Esquire the Third, do you hear the words of this great depressed man? Do you recognize your likeness in his eyes?" But you're drunk again, cursing out a kidney pie in pig Latin. I look to Johnson for solace, but he laughs, pinching wheat-stained vermin from under my wig, soberly addressing one at close range. "And thee," he says, "I shall name Boswell."

Mary Shelley

The Villa Diodati, when vegetation rioted on earth at the mere hip-hop of a harp, and the genital spirit was more than just a medium-rare idea. I give two thumbs down to angry love, I give it an Everlasting Nay! "So dramatic," you say. You boast that you've "discovered" Woman, so consider this question: "When a virgin marries a river, who plays at the reception?" Love is like this, my boy. We talk of young girls with red pony tails, sipping from pink champagne glasses impaled with tiny orange umbrellas. "Be not, let not, take heed," I warn. "Do not beat me with your heart-shaped club, your silly ideas, half-distinguished and persistent as a procession of ants. . . ." The Villa Diodati where everyone is sick of Byron, even the Monster. "Her smile, how persuasive it was, and how pathetic!" That's Percy. "If you were to have someone whip you, whom would you choose?" That's Byron. "I will be a good girl and never vex you more." That's Mary. How we'd like to hear those words, at night, in the study by candlelight. She's a woman with a mind, no slight blot on this Promethean landscape where every man is hung like a centaur, or thinks he is. "What are you talking about?" you ask . . . Let's peek in on Sleeping Mary as she dreams of groves and corpses, of young Victor crouched over his creation, of the Villa Diodati itself, where tomorrow the Monster will once again lurch from her pen, while Shelley's and Byron's "I" and "Me" wrestle into the early morning hours.

Freud

"If it wasn't for pickpockets, Sigmund wouldn't have any sex life at all." That's not funny, that's not original. "Unsatisfactory Citizenship" on your report card. That's not funny, either. Or smoking pot. Or bookmarking G-spots on the Internet. I swear, if you snuck outside to fart, the wind would blow it back in. Sigmund, You the Man. A little help, please. Cure this Oedipal itch, marinade this meathead . . . Freud, old and quiet, sipping from a whitebone coffee mug adorned with the image of the Sphinx. He's mourning a lost dream, picking a piece of lint from his beard. Nearby, the famous couch covered with an oriental rug. I can smell its horsehair stuffing, I can smell his cigar. "Humbaba, Humbaba," you mumble, attracting his attention with a Gilgameshic mantra. You plan to manufacture a key ring in the shape of a brooch bearing the face of this bearded old man. "Humbaba, Humbaba." "That's not funny," I say, then get distracted by a flamboyant entrance. It's Wilhelm Fliess, alias Chard deNose, commissioned to explore your corpora cavernosa, a phrase you'd understand if you ever flashed your flash cards. "Ain't got no biorhythms," you say, "ain't got no self-control. Can't even dance." But Fliess will have none of it. He has you strapped to the couch, giving you a fascist facial, poking at a mound of nasal flesh with a sharp scalpel. "I'll give you Humbaba," he says, as Freud looks on, toying with a thick piece of gauze.

Hemingway

I was writing a play called *Nada*. You were interested in "Grace under pressure," thinking it was a sex act . . . "Papa, do you mind if I call you Daddy?" Which, of course, is a tautology—a word Hemingway would have hated, along with "favonian" and "focine," though they were good enough for Vladimir N. . . . Pamplona! The running of the bulls. "Airnesto?" I say, with a phony Andalusian accent. He's standing in the middle of a two-room flat, wearing tan shorts and a blood-red apron with "Born to Fish" etched in white. I'm leaning out a window, watching a posse of hungover aficionados with red hoof prints, like birthmarks, on their backs. Yesterday, for a brief moment, everyone was a pugilist. "Someday," Ernesto says, "someone will place a gun in my hand and say, 'Follow your instincts.' Meanwhile, can't eat, can't drink, can't fuck." "But you're a good cook," I say. And he is! This Ernesto is an old Ernesto—his thin white hair combed forward, his love-horn filed and shaved down like that of a half-bull. I say, "We all could use one of those wiry ballbusters you wrote about, some freckled-face, red-headed expatriate who'll appear at the front door, swearing like a storm trooper and hugging a weatherbeaten wine flask." He smiles, then extracts a live ten-inch trout from a metal pail, knocking it unconscious with a head butt. Suddenly, the twang of an acoustic guitar, and you enter from the bathroom, naked except for a hand towel the size of a fig leaf. You're delirious with fever, half-believing you've been bull-wounded. "Jasmine's neck has finally healed from the bite of that German shepherd," you announce, which comment piques this here picador—meaning me. But Ernesto's elated and throws the wet trout against a whiskey-stained wall. "Antonio, Antonio," he moans, removing his red apron, making an artful pass at you.

Malcolm X

"White America is doomed!" Finally, a statement we agree with.

"If I were black, I know I'd be angry." "You're always angry, anyway," you say. And I am. I am the angriest white man in America. I shoot people the finger for adjusting their rearview mirrors, I curse into the hollow ears of telemarketers . . . Mid-twentieth century, Malcolm's eighth grade teacher lecturing, "You've got to be realistic about being a nigger, Malcolm." And Malcolm thinks: *By any means necessary!* . . . Two blocks down, our resident skinhead rearranges his collection of human skulls, says he can prove white superiority by measuring the distance between his navel and penis. "I am the reincarnation of Hitler," he announces. "I come from the planet Zeno." And Malcolm says, "By any means necessary!" And: "When people are angry, they are not interested in logic, they are not interested in odds, they are not interested in consequences." Jimmy Reed was angry, just back from Nam with pink pills, blue pills, white pills, all wrapped in a ball of tin foil. One night two tons of steel rods dropped from his overhead crane. "Maybe he wasn't angry," you say, "maybe just tired." And now, ladies and gentleman, time for a few white, liberal anecdotes—about your one black friend who took you to your first rap concert ("dog, it was phat"); about your one black friend who dated your sister ("he was a gentleman"); about your one black friend who got drunk with you under a midnight sky illuminated by sparks from the steel plant ("he called me Brother"). "White, blue-eyed devil." "Two-legged snake." "White ape and beast." We are all of these—even you, my tow-headed, green-eyed gangsta boy, with a black, silk bandanna around your head, lip-syncing lyrics of a Wu-Tang song predicting your doom.

When Malcolm was shot, some cops were sleeping, others playing three-card monte in the men's room. *By any means necessary!* Malcolm would have shouted.

Maharishi Yogi

I have a mantra. It sounds like *άιμα,* the Greek word for blood. I want to be a Swami but I talk too much. I mean to say, I don't listen, I cut people off. Last week my main chakra was out of whack—rattling like a tambourine. My *Fana* was famished. When someone says, "The true seeing is when there is no seeing," I get a headache. Tomorrow I'll change my mantra to *But,* yours to *Yet.* At least then we'll be honest. I'd break Descartes' kneecaps if I could, he's the real troublemaker. So very loud in his Land of Self—opposites rubbing shoulders, chanting, or doing a sexy dance. "Manure worm." "Navel Gazer." We gladly embrace these insults. "I exhale next to plants," you laugh. "I do my best to stay poor." For that wisecrack, I proclaim you my Sherpa companion. You will be in charge of my yak herd. Your new name will be Chucklehead.

> *Master: The dead will return in taxi cabs.*
> *Disciple: But, Master, there are no taxi cabs in Khembalung.*
> *Master: Which is why the dead will return.*

I'm getting better at this. Yesterday, I sat still for an hour. I took twenty minutes to pee. It was a kind of meditation.

Return

End of the twentieth century and I'm still angry. The new hero same as the old hero. And the poets? They're out back playing in the wet mulch, writing each other love letters with bird shit on brown paper bags. Just want to don my pajamas and curl up with a good book, but there aren't any. "Take it easy, Lady Philosophy," you warn. "Whoa there, Mr. Negativity." You're pointing to your souvenirs: jodhpurs from Jodhpur, an artificial ass from the court of Louis XIV, an eyelash of Catherine the Great. I shave my head, put on my swim cap limed with Bengay. I sit in a corner, sifting through the ashes of famous people. It's a metaphor, gentle reader. It's not a metaphor, gentle reader. Like everyone else, we wanted to become a legend, or a footnote to an obscure anecdote. We were driven by the certainty of heavy soil and that starlet's buttock. And I wanted to *educate* you, and would have, if the cockroaches hadn't eaten our canoe. There was certainly no ostriching on my part; I faced down every truth, every falsehood. "On my trip I met a woman named DNA," you croon with that silly look on your face, then ask to play outside with the Famous Poet, who's holding a sacred fish over his head, saying, "When the hook is caught in the lower jaw that means your vahine has been unfaithful." This is not a metaphor, gentle reader. Not even a Strange Fact of the Week Just a little jab to keep us moving, to keep us on the run . . .

This cave—my sadsick head—everyone fixed on a dark day
when Death's face shone forth like a show dog's wet nose.
For once the eye before the "I." "Try to keep busy," Eduardo
says, wanting to cheer me up. "Stalk a beautiful girl, stroke
her red hair, praise the curve of her shoulders in a hastily-
learned foreign language." "Forget the girl," I say. "Forget the
TV, especially." "How 'bout them ghosts," he chants, my head
about to explode. And here's Mother Earth with fiery celes-
tial balls bearing down on her; here's the American Sphinc-
ter Muscle as loose as a goose. "I'm talking about fear, Edu-
ardo, about doomsday devices which may or may not exist."
"Fly, then, false shadows of Hope, I shall chase thee no more."
What drama queen said that? Nowadays we'd settle for a
second-hand miracle, like last night on the outdoor patio,
munching corn chips and guacamole, no fuel-filled planes
overhead, no skunks hiding in the bushes. Voluptuaries of all
ages, of every species and sex: "Welcome!" And this is how
we spend our days . . .

II

Eduardo, wash that finger if you plan to cook tonight . . . I always wanted a friend, even an enemy, named Eduardo. I'd show him off to people, cause a ruckus. Create a chaos like an upswelling of a well—really swirling . . . Before we left the cleaners we got the bad news: skunks had caused a landslide at the dumpster. There I stood, beat-up cat carrier in one hand, trusty nine-iron in the other. This could've been my much-anticipated photo op, but Eduardo had left the camera at home. He stood behind a grimy milk truck, carving out WASH ME with his right index finger. Which might suggest Eduardo is a punk. But he is not. Eduardo is my friend. Eduardo is my enemy.

Eduardo thinks he's Bukowski. Even wants to be called Buk. He's shaved his head and glued a misshapen rubber ball to his nose, poured flesh-colored warm wax over his face, kneaded it like dough. Then a fake beard, a moustache, and a black Dracula fright wig. "Love's a dog from hell," he says, "and so I walk up to this fag poet and say 'Hey, Little Dick, take a sip of this.'" Eduardo hands me his bottle of tomato juice, mumbles, "That's right, motherfucker." Later, I find him crying over a *Baywatch* episode, the one where Mitch goes temporarily blind. Most of his makeup's melted, little of note except some bagel crumbs around his lips. He knows he should be sulking in a beat-up Ford Falcon outside the girls' Catholic high school, playing with himself as the dismissal bell sounds. He knows he should be helping some whore shoot up in her neck. But for Eduardo, just a little *Baywatch,* a bagel and tomato juice—cream cheese on the side.

VIII

I judge a theodicy by the slant of its jaw, by how quickly my bowels act up, by the red apple resting on the bleached blonde's head. (Read "question" for "head," "answer" for "apple"). Get it, you naive divinity students of archery, second-rate *hamartians,* always missing the mark? And here's Eduardo, dressed in spandex American flag bicycle shorts and a delicate red T-shirt. One black skate engraved with a white YES, one white skate with a black NO. He's discovered theodicy in the Roller Derby. The Elvis of Elbow Jabs, the Wizard of Whips. He's one tough cookie. Far from the Eduardo we discovered sitting on the toilet with a plastic bag over his head. So many Eduardos, it's hard to know who's the real one, so just keep moving, trail his sorry ass around a plywood oval track, listen to the roar from his tattooed, multiple-pierced, spike-heeled groupies. No 1970s flashback here, just Eduardo making a point, jammin' with the best of them. "S-A-T-U-R-D-A-Y N-I-G-H-T," the announcer bellows, dropping a blood-red handkerchief onto the track. They're off!

Eduardo has a ringing in his ears; before he knows it, there's an orchestra, the shock of a hundred triangles simultaneously struck. Doctor Doctors blame the inner ear of his inner child, or maybe just a wacky jaw joint. Nothing to do but wire that jaw shut, teach him self-hypnosis. "It's all in your head," they say, which makes Inner Eddie sad. All day he stares at a sky-blue plaster wall, drinking protein shakes through a plastic straw, a suspiciously feminine voice wooing him to sleep. You have to pity him. You have to loathe those Doctor Doctors, or want to tug hard on their pointed beards. Man, they're killing Eddie's inner music. "Bird, prune thy wing! Nightingale, sing," I whisper, and within a week, he's sashaying na-ked among the backyard tulips. "Mama Doctors, Papa Doctors, please let this Eddie boogie-woogie, 'cause it's in him, and it's gotsa come out."

XII

Speaking of which … who hasn't been someone else in another life? Not Eduardo, who always was and always will be. "I yam what I yam," he yokes, while shredding his black birth certificate. Now there's an image with a rough wood-grain feel to it. Today's motif is Death, which I signal by waving my black, faux-bamboo fedora with a white NO! embroidered on the brim. Speaking of which … it's not true our minivan fell off the lift, damaging Eduardo's head. He wasn't even in the vicinity. We were in the waiting room, reading old copies of *National Geographic*, Eddie as happy as the wet water buffalo on the front cover, giddy as an air hose infatuated with its own flatulence. Someone had handed him a five-dollar bill, which he gave to me. "You will be blessed if you pass this on," was scribbled in red ink, but there was just the two of us, so I passed it back. "Put 'The Power' to work," I said, waiting for the fiver to come my way. So I repeat: let Death be today's motif, our guiding participle, henceforth appearing in italics, like the letters on a gravestone Eddie and I once imagined.

Eduardo is writing a memoir, which is hard to do when you have no memories—a revelation that demands explanation: the real dope from a real dope. A rainy afternoon and I was seriously bored—real lonely, man. And I had run out of booze. You get the picture? Eddie's reading from a tiny notebook he stole from my briefcase: "I was born," he sighs, "near the weed-infested drive-in next to the abandoned shopping mall, my first memory being a blast of lightning, then a great headsin, as impenetrable as an Incan convent." More and more ridiculous images drenched in disappointment and despair, ending with the "red cushion on the family sleigh." "Cut the cheesy drama," I say, perfectly aware of the "red cushion" and of every birdbrain who ever tweeted in the family tree. This memoir could use a good whipping, a black belt whipping, or just forget the whole thing—don our homemade coconut caps and sip iced tea on our newly painted front porch. Wait to be nighted, then awake at sunrise to the thunk of a newspaper against our broken screen door.

XV

Be it acknowledged that when Mexican gods are bored, they get tat-
tooed . . . Unable to derive satisfaction in the usual ways, we agreed
upon something artificial. Eddie took the lead. The man *does* have cour-
age, and I'd have never found Rusty Needle without him, nor met the
Ivy League girl with a tomato-sized ladybug tattooed on her ass. We
had decided to edit an anthology of poets with tattoos on their toes.
"We can begin with my twin brother Ralph," Eddie joked, as I bared my
massive big toe, nearly making the Ivy League girl pop out of her pants.
"Ouch!" I yelled, but it all ended up fine: the Ivy Leaguer patting my
head, hypnotizing me with her oyster shell necklace, murmuring, "Huzza,
huzza," as the metal made its mark—Rusty Needle grinning like a hula
dancer, everything fine until Eduardo said to cool it with the bad similes.
But I was into it now, sweaty, all revved up like a hurricane, my Ivy Leagu-
er aroused, anxious as a winded poodle that just lost its little red bow.

XVII

"There's an electricity that's hard to describe," my pony-tailed waiter explains. He's really Eduardo, with a tattoo of a half moon on his forehead, a huge sapphire pendant around his neck. But I'm barely listening, scanning the dessert menu, taking notes. They're out of cheesecake, carrot cake, mud pie, too, and Eduardo swears he can heal with his hands. "Oh, the night, the night," he croons, "when the wind full of welkin feeds our faces." He's been to The Other Side, slept with a girl whose brother's ex-girlfriend went down on Elvis. Such proximity to the Great One is dizzying. "It's like he's in the room," he says. But not even a chocolate croissant in this place, so I pocket my pen, drape my raincoat over my head, dodge raindrops the size of crickets. Tonight, we'll listen to "Heartbreak Hotel," imagine Elvis soiling himself on stage, firing two .45s into the ceiling and television—his favorite book the Physician's Desk Reference, his favorite expression, "Better to be unconscious than miserable." But for now, our socks are wet, our stomachs hurt—only the green lights of the gay coffee shop between us and home. Curiosity leads us on.

XIX

To hang upside down from the top of the Biltmore at 4 a.m. with no possibility of applause. That's what Eduardo wants, then to work his way toward prime time, 5 p.m., when a crowd colonizes and is hungry for a happening. Perhaps remove his black silk blindfold and shout obscenities, drop cat-eyed marbles onto the crowd, spin with arms outstretched in mock crucifixion. "I saw the best minds of my generation destroyed by madness," he'll say, knowing someone's already said that, knowing everything's already been said. But he's not dismayed. He's wearing his lucky underwear, hanging upside down from the top of the Biltmore. A great day ahead of him! A great life!

XXI

We're starting a band, a real ass-kicking, girl-licking kind of thing. "My axe is the most powerful instrument in the world," Eduardo says, fingering his Les Paul with one hand, snapping the pink bra strap of his fourteen-year-old girlfriend with the other. "God damn," he yells, chug-a-lugging a bottle of Jack Daniel's. "God damn this wondrous life." God damn, for sure, I think, watching him tongue the girl's nose earring, as she drifts into a drunken prepubescent sleep. Yes, music fans, it's girls, girls, girls, when all I wondered was whether you had to be a jerk to be a rock star. Because we sure is that. "Pass the loco weed," I say to a middle-aged redhead turntabling naked in the middle of the floor, no doubt wondering why her red go-go boots are nailed over the fireplace. Blow on my harmonica, that's what I'll do. Chatter in scat. I got no real words for this Vicodin moment, just a few blue notes mixing with the groans of a multitude of groupies. "Drop dead old man," someone yells from a pile of flesh. It's Eduardo, who's decided to name us The Eduardo Experience—a two-jerk band, noted for its obscurity . . .

XXIV

Sometimes I'm cruel to Eduardo, sometimes embrace him gently like a porcupine. So it goes with one's worst self. You could say, "Eduardo's the one things happen to," or "I don't know which one of us has written this page." But that would be someone else's poem, someone else's nightmare. You could say, "God bless Eduardo, he lived like a rat," but, in fact, Eddie lives quite well, with little responsibility: Lots of steaks on the grill and fairways cut short for great backspin; lots of girls if he wants them, and he does, and he doesn't, and he does. Life's loud and unruly when he's around, though not much better when he's not. I'll miss his books of torture, his tiny oval pills, his two fish darting in opposite directions. But we know he has to go—"though remember," he warns, "I shall be with you on your wedding night," then leaps onto an ice-covered raft, disappearing into the frozen darkness of my skull . . .

Overture

I'm sick of peekaboo metaphors, weary of mad stabs at uncertainty. And there's a guy making fun of my name, a nasty little prick with a Polaroid moment stuck in his head—his mother cheering as another perfect number two vanishes down the drain. So I go next store and order the Stud Muffin sandwich. Try to be friends with my son, talk about responsibility, always responsibility, watch his fingers tighten around a butter knife. And here's a joke laden with loot: We bought a little pug to forget about the TV. We volunteered to open the neighborhood mail, to take deep breaths. It ain't easy training a dog. It ain't easy living with all this cruelty. For example: How many people have I wished dead? None. How many injured? None. How many have made me sad? A great many. I count them while trying to fall asleep. And how's your Reuben? I ask. And how's your Stud Muffin? he asks back, then homeward where we take the pug for a walk, not talking, momentarily distracted by one of those ellipses which make certain historians want to slash their wrists.

Trees

How many things can you say about a tree? How many times compare it to our crummy lives, stretch the metaphor until its esophagus bursts, or bleeds? We cut down our trees. Nothing symbolic about that. The baby raccoons were using them to climb onto the roof and torture me with their pretty faces. "Let me be," I screamed, as they scratched the screen, wanting to lick or maybe even eat me. I couldn't sleep for days, for weeks. I watched the spidery limbs of trees shadowboxing on my bedroom wall, as if something was grieving in them, as if they wanted to be put out of their misery, as if they were saying, "Make it look like an accident." But if by "accident" we mean that which comes without cause or design, there is really no such thing. That's something God would have said, or one of His half-baked philosophers, and they would have been right, for it was indeed my landscaper-cousin who sawed those pretty logs you see drying in the sun, who drove those raccoons away. "Sleep quietly, dry logs," I whisper, before retiring at night, then don my earphones, listening to an overweight actor recite some righteous Wordsworthian iambs.

The Half-Full, Half-Empty Episode

A car that's a bass guitar rattles my windows—a ritual I run my life by unless someone knocks on the door. No one ever knocks on the door. Hello from the City where the natives drive little cars with big antennae, where pedestrians lug enormous "I"s on their backs. "As a man thinketh, so he is." But I ain't been thinketh so good lately, indecisive as a blind switchboard operator with two left hands. Hello from the City where it's morning, where the rain-washed speeding traffic can make a snake nervous. "Hallelujah!" I yell, tripping over annotated self-help manuals strewn across the floor—then dead-headed by the sight of two long-stemmed roses peeking over a windowsill, by a saxophone singing in the distance, by the hickory smell of bacon. "The correct answer," my wife explains, "is that the glass contains water." Hello from the City where certainty can be found in a rose, in the burnt portion of a cheese omelet, in the matching yellow headbands of two long-stemmed roses, in a lousy glass of water.

Bang!

Yesterday I wondered why the blacks weren't rioting. Even I want to shorten the days of most white people I meet. Funny, how we're not supposed to say things like that—instead, slip into our iron shoes, stumble past each other as if we don't exist until my kid puts a .22 cartridge into the palm of your kid and shouts, "Bang!" Today our smug city streets are coated with ice, a few orphaned birds cling to frozen branches. I trod down to the park, anticipating The Final Showdown, which of course never comes—just a biting February chill, like a February thirty years ago when I got stoned in a railroad car with Jimmy Reed. We were waiting for the crane to arrive and drop its chains. Later, at the Governor's Inn, Buddy Guy was playing. Jimmy said to hang close, cup my hand over my beer, "Don't stare." I was eighteen, two years older than my son, who goes to school with kids of every race and color, yet hangs with his own—mostly blond and blue-eyed boys, tapping their toes to the angry bass of rap, mouthing misogynies while Little League trophies tremble on their dressers.

Hawk

Sometimes I awake with a headline stuck in my head—Doctor in Bangor Treating Elvis for Migraines; Pharmacist Completes History of Drive-In Movie Theater—and I write it all down in my little red notebook. But there are other nights when blood rocks my heart, and people I've injured or the dead appear, hovering above the ceiling fan. The city is asleep, the city is awake, the city is napping. Does it matter? I think, climbing insomnia's creaky stairs to an attic that doesn't exist, trying to remember what is good, what is right. Yesterday, my student fell from a tree and died. That morning I knelt before the dog's crate and kissed her goodbye. I stopped to buy cough drops and a backscratcher. I was cut off twice and beeped at once. My student wrote a story about the Civil War, about heroism. He wrote about an uprising of Christmas reindeer, about a boy and his imaginary camel. He drew a cartoon called the "Devolution of Man," and he once wrote: "Artists have to try, no matter how hard, to love their enemy because it is up to artists to save humanity." Because he believed in what he wrote, he wasn't my best writer. He wasn't a liar, he wasn't waiting for applause. The clap of crows emptying a tree was enough for him, the simple architecture of an egg. He had climbed, I think, to gain a different perspective, like the hawk that mysteriously appeared today. I was walking to class and sensed its dracular presence, then heard a squirrel's lament no more than ten feet away—a bone-crushing sorrow for life, for death.

Massaging the Ass of a Pregnant Woman

Hail to the leaf, to the bleeding milk of dandelions, to the boulder under which an ant is eating its enemy! Even to computer carcasses piled high in a red pickup, to raccoons kneeling before a nearby dumpster. "Where to begin?" I ask Quaamina, my Hindu guide, master in the art of pressing flesh. "Personal hygiene counts one-half of one per cent," he reminds me, though it's hard to hear over the wall chatter of our Monet haystacks, over an elastic sobbing in my sock drawer. It seems a pack of extra large condoms feels left out. No! It's an unsheathed Swiss Army knife wreaking havoc on a handkerchief. No! Just a backyard door slamming, then a few grunts from the neighbor's above-ground pool. "From the beginning," I say, "I refused to leave the womb—the bright lights, the doctors promising I'd be a girl." But let's return to the clanking overhead fan, to our extra firm mattress, to the familiar flesh between finger and thumb. "Time to dig in," Quaamina says smiling. "Wasn't it she, after all, who invented the sigh?"

Neighbors

Street prophet, soothsayer, stargazer extraordinaire. In fact, he's the local loony dressed in a red beret, sky-blue shirt and red pants. Every day the same outfit, pacing the same sidewalk, mumbling to himself or swearing at passersby as if his balls are on fire. One day he screamed at my infant and made him cry. "The next time," I said, "I'll kill you." I told him to imagine a noose swinging from the tree he was leaning on. "I'll lynch you," I yelled. Quite surprisingly, we became good friends. I can't make sense of his mumbling, yet follow him with the baby jogger every Sunday as he eviscerates cans of garbage lining our street. He's collecting doomsday articles, one about strangelets, tiny cosmic missiles that weigh tons and travel at 900,000 miles per hour, yet are only the size of pollen grain. In 1993 one entered the Earth in Antarctica and blasted out 23 seconds later in the Indian Ocean. No wonder he ducks a lot, and why bother changing your clothes when a little ball bearing might tear a tiny hole in your head, exiting your left testicle one nanosecond later. I explain this phenomenon to an old guy walking his nasty black mongrel. A year ago, his dog leapt out of nowhere, snapping at us. "I'm going to kill your dog," I yelled, which made us enemies for a very long time. But now he tags along—three wise men, amusing ourselves as the Earth takes a terrible beating.

Poor, Poor Pitiful Me

Meanwhile back at the branch, the long-awaited return of the cardinal while two saxophones butt heads in a nearby warehouse . . . City, my city! I've spent all day raking leaves from last fall, dodging two yellow jackets that haven't learned how to avoid people. But I have. Even in a neighborhood where prowlers pee in our backyard, or leave behind condoms and Dunkin' Donut bags. Today, I scattered rocks at the base of our fence. At night I opened our bedroom window, waiting to hear a tibia's sweet crack from the creep who broke my driver's side window, stealing our Linda Ronstadt CD. Thirty years ago, when he stole *Santana Abraxis*—the same guy, I swear it—I taped razor blades to the base of my 8-track stereo, one night forgetting the genius of the idea and shredding my calf while mounting a woman I would love but not marry. Meanwhile, somewhere in the country—Simplicity: an old man in his bathroom shaking off his penis for the fifth time, his granddaughter asleep on the back porch, watching stars flame up in a minute-by-minute account of the universe. Somewhere moose and little beasties run wild, while people sleep soundly, deliriously happy to be part of Nature's puny plan. But I'm happy, too, gripping the handle of a pellet gun, crouched half asleep beneath my bedroom window, humming the lyrics to "Poor, Poor Pitiful Me."

Snails

I admire the brute dampness of snails. I ate them once in a little restaurant outside Toronto. A medium-sized war was going on, and I was dating a girl I skipped school for. We'd go to the zoo and watch the orangutans regurgitate. We'd toss peanuts to the elephants or wave to giraffes, hoping for their approval. Sometimes we'd end up in Canada, cubes of hash hidden in the studs of our jeans as my '59 Rambler American lurched across the border. Unlike most stories, this one's true, full of youth and trouble, but mostly confusion, especially about God, whom I began calling "God the Forgetful," saddened that one baby could be born armless, another with two heads. It had become hard to like God, or depend on Him for the simplest chores. Even now wars rage on, babies still exploding from wombs minus arms and legs. You can't even turn on TV without hearing someone's daughter explain to a wide-eyed audience how she had sex with nine guys and one woman to earn money for a home entertainment center. Makes me want to revert to Plan B. Makes me wonder why I'm back in Toronto, outside a jazz club, eating snails, watching an unmarked aircraft descend upon the city.

The Whole Truth

The truth is I was a fat child, boring as meatloaf. The truth is I was a skinny child with a "very special glow." Take your pick. We make it up as we go along. Not like our baby who spent the last fifteen minutes placing a coaster on top of a cup, trying to make a connection. When I was a fat child I always knew what was behind Door Number One, even when a waitress thought my family was black and refused to seat us. It was 1959 with spiders as big as marbles patrolling our summer cottage. It was 1959, I just a skinny kid with a big appetite who laughed and laughed. What were you? you're probably screaming by now. But you're missing the point. Like when my friend said, "Wherever there are birds there are birdwatchers." Really? Who says you have to see something for it to exist? I remember my divorced-dad drives home, when I cried into the steering wheel and considered driving off the road or directly into another divorced-dad, or when I was so broke I couldn't afford an oil change or a new pair of shoes. Is that spirit-filled, low-down, and pathetic enough truth for you? The truth is I live in the ultimate guy pad with a small cache of automatic weapons hidden under a homemade shrine to St. Jude. All day I nap and read the great classics, sometimes watering my plants. I cry at golf events and pray to be the last swallowed headfirst at The Final Showdown. An incredible world, my world! Whatever you can imagine, whatever you can stand.

Explanation

What should I tell you? That it rained for five straight days, that our gutters leaked in spite of the duct tape, that a rat ate through the cellar screen and killed our cat? Today, a bus exploded in Israel killing eighteen people, and no one is paying attention. We pour our oatmeal, cover it with bran, with raisins. We rev up our stainless steel juicers and kiss each other goodbye. "In a brazen daytime ambush yesterday," I read, then feed the dog, take her for a walk. It's been one year since the world was silenced by a ringing in my ears, my jaw tightening at the thought of leaving home. Gone was the trail left by any stupid thought. Gone the long conversations with friends on the phone, or killing time with a raisin bagel in a loud coffee shop with absolutely no fear of being blown into another galaxy, one much saner than ours. But I got used to the ringing, just as I get used to the headlines, to the lies and counter lies, barely audible over the bad music of the nightly news, over Sunday sermons as useless as a clock we once buried inside a snowman's brainless head—its tick, tick, ticking. "As an armor-plated bus lumbered up the winding road to Emanuel," I read. "As a powerful bomb exploded, riddling the vehicle with shrapnel. . . ."

Just Listen

I sit by the window and watch a great mythological bird go down in flames. In fact, it's a kite the neighborhood troublemaker has set on fire. Twenty-one and still living at home, deciding when to cut through a screen and chop us into little pieces. "He wouldn't hurt a fly," his mother would say, as they packed our parts into black antiseptic body bags. I explain this possibility to the garbage men. I'm trying to make friends with them, unable to understand why they leave our empty cans in the middle of the driveway, then laugh as they walk away. One says, "Another name for moving air is wind, and shade is just a very large shadow"—perhaps a nice way to make me feel less eclipsed. It's not working, it's not working. I'm scared for children yet to be abducted, scared for the pregnant woman raped at knife point on the New Jersey Turnpike, scared for what violence does to one's life, how it squats inside the hollow heart like a dead cricket. My son and his friends found a dead cricket, coffined it in a plastic Easter egg and buried it in the backyard. It was a kind of time capsule, they explained—a surprise for some future boy archeologist, someone much happier than us, who will live during a time when trees don't look so depressed, and birds and dogs don't chatter and growl like the chorus in an undiscovered Greek tragedy.

I Know You're Probably Sick of Me

You're probably thinking, "This guy should cheer up." Or you'd like to glare at me and say, "Have a little faith, Bucko, stop complaining." I see your point. I've never heard an elephant moan, "I'm lonely, so lonely," or a seal whine, "It's not fair." On the very last episode of *The Slayer*, Buffy said, "The battle between good and evil isn't about wishes, it's about choices"—words that haunt me as I mail my check for *A Short Course in Miracles*, then take my infant to the zoo. At his age an elephant might as well be a monkey, but he's happy to be somewhere outside himself. According to *A New Catechism*, "a miracle is an event occurring outside of nature," yet I'm happiest when pouring concrete or changing a diaper, when listening to the outdoor zapper fry hundreds of virus-infested mosquitoes. You're probably thinking, "Back off, pal. Take a pill." But how much safer we'd feel if God were a car mechanic or a drunk—anything to suggest He's working and suffering like the rest of us. Granted, not the happiest thoughts for the zoo, and who wants to piss off God, though I know He'll love me, even be amused, when I stand before Him, saying, "I tried, I tried"—not sure whether I really did.

One Hell of a Year

I've had one hell of a year and wonder when I'll have to pay for it, which is why I still wear my "New Dad" bracelet, which got me free parking and unlimited lousy coffee in the hospital cafeteria. I hold my infant close to my breast. I take him wherever I go. Who's going to whack a guy with a baby, who's going to say, "Give me your wallet, or I'll bust you up?" What kind of God would have man and child run down by a Mack truck, or crushed by a load of steel meant for the new Children's Museum? Even got some poems read this year and won a big award. Got to play with my wife in a hotel we could've never afforded. Got to New York, New York, where the food at the reception was great. And to the poet who said I mispronounced "Laughlin," I suggest a frontal lobotomy with a rusty screwdriver. And to the poet who said, "No one reads John Berryman anymore," I offer cement shoes and a bridge in Minneapolis to leap from. And to the poet who said … But, ah, this is a happy poem about the wonderful year I've had, which I know I'll have to pay for because that's how it works: a leaky cell phone, the old bone-in-the-throat gag, caught with my pants down at the Bill Clinton Motor Lodge, dead-headed by a socket wrench at 1 a.m. in the Cumberland Farms parking lot. But, again, let's sing a happy poem for my one hell of a year—for endless nights in damp and twisted sheets, or a simple cup of chai as I sit on my front porch, listening to my teenage son tell the whole damn neighborhood how much he loves me.

Houdini Weenie

For this trick, a time machine, a little ore dust, and a smoke-stack staining the sky with chemicals. Add a fat boy, locked in his room while a party's rip-and-roar rattles holy statues on his dresser. It's me, gentle reader, sent to bed for shattering McMahon's picture window, for eating the coconut icing before the first "Happy Birthday" broke wind, for calling aunt Esther an alien and having the goods to prove it. Through a crack in the door, I see her husband in cherry-red flip-flops, polishing his glasses with a tissue, smiling at this here unfortunate peeper. Earlier that day I read a book on Galileo. I was hooked on telescopes, searching for the magic ring concealed in cereal boxes of skinny boys, of boys with money and pedigreed dogs. It's the late 1950s, and through a screened bedroom window, I see a full moon shot full of holes. And through a screened bedroom window I tumble, caught an hour later stealing candy from a local drugstore. "A regular escape artist," my uncle says, shaking his finger at me. "A regular little Houdini Weenie."

Neil

On the corner, two guys arguing over a can a beer. I want to break open a box of cartridges but don't own a gun. I want to complain to my dead friend Neil, who would say, "Smile, it's a good day to be Peter." I think of Neil as I awake to the Latino's La Cucaracha horn at 6 a.m., or shake off my penis for the fifth time in the middle of the night, or wrestle with a wet diaper, then stand in the rain as if stoned while the dog takes a crap. This is a life Neil may have glimpsed before being headonned by an ice-covered pine tree. I envied him that rush, though I was angry, so sad even my fingernails hurt. I can see his wife stumbling down the carpeted aisle, flanked by two Labrador retrievers, a life-sized picture of Neil on the altar—later, the dogs howling outside like two bruised saxophones while the cheese dip got passed around. I knew very few people in that church. How could that be? So here I am, a little hungover, listening to two guys argue over a can of beer. Across the hall, a little boy named Lucas stirs in his toddler bed, unable to imagine the many ways people can die. "It's a good day to be Lucas," Neil would've told him. "It's a good day to tell your father you love him."

American Male, Acting Up

They say your whole life flashes before you when you die, but I'm sure I'll witness the lives of others. And if I'm right, please spare me the lives of this bearded oaf in a black wife-beater, mid-calf jeans, and orange work boots. We're at the zoo, more precisely the habitat of the arctic fox, whom we've never seen awake, terminally depressed to find himself in a moderately-sized ethnically-mixed city surrounded by creatures who hurl animal crackers, caw like crows, or scream, "Wake up, stupid," which is what this man's two boys are yelling. When I tell my two-year-old to ignore them, he asks, "Why?" and I say, "Because anyone with half a brain wouldn't scare a little fox." The man glares at me, and I glimpse the chaos of his past lives. It is the feast of Saturnalia. He smells of grapes and cheese, the blood of his Thracian slave hardened on his left thigh. He's swigging diluted wine, exchanging arm punches with friends. He's the hirsute sweat bag movies portray with thumb downturned, the one who two thousand years later chugs four beers, then goes to the zoo to torment the animals. Laugh if you must, but I would gladly take this bully down. So when he stares, I stare back, and when he says, "Boys, we paid our money, so scream whatever you want," I brace myself, prepare to take a beating.

Cheerleader

There it was: the cheerleader outfit my wife wore when she was seventeen, and how saddened not to be the first to take it off—behind a bush, in the back seat of a car, on a beach chair next to Joe Blow's swimming pool. I wanted to punish her with questions, make the peach fuzz quiver on her cheeks, force her to read my friend's penny dreadful novel. I imagined her by a water fountain, posing for some halfwit hockey player. "What could be simpler than to Think Pink," she would say—Old Halfwit stunned still, rooted to the cheap linoleum floor. I imagined the middle-aged Math teacher's front-row grin as she performed her famous mid-air split. Our living-room rug was small consolation, worn in spots from hands and knees. Not even my little book of love poems eased the pain. "And by the way," I say to her twenty years later, "of course they respect you for your mind, so ignore their groans when you bend to retrieve a pencil, or reach for a file on top of your desk."

I've Tried To Like Poets

I've tried to like poets, gone to readings, hugged them, said things like, "Yes, poets are problematic, but the best of them are the very best people you'll ever meet," then gone home and downed a shot of antacid. Do poets really care about poetry, or are they in it for those readings when they bed a wide-eyed graduate student in her deepest moment of sadness, while all she wanted was to be hugged, to share the motel's continental breakfast with a guy with half a brain? How to trust the tongue and lips of a poet bent on getting bent, even that phrase enough to excite the anorexic heiress who chose The Word instead of leaping off a bridge. But as I said, "The best poets are the very best people you'll ever meet," especially if you've been imprisoned for a number of years. "Now that's not nice," my nice self says, the one who's trying very hard to like poets, who hugs them at readings, pecks them playfully on the cheek, who holds them down when they awaken trembling and half crazy in the early morning hours in a Motel 6 far from home.

And Nothing Else Matters

On I-395 between Occum and Preston the interstate ablaze with foliage, a heavy metal ballad swelling the speakers of my SUV, I weep like the middle-aged fool I am. My wife called me from Hartford to say Sue Anne overdosed in a motel in North Carolina when she was supposed to be alive in a motel in White Plains. Supposedly because of a man, which is another way of saying *Fate*. Supposedly because of her mother, which is another way of saying *Love*. *Whoever is sick will become well. Whoever is well will become sick*. If I credit this passage to Aquinas, will it console you? Will you drive to North Carolina and empty Sue Anne's belongings into a cardboard box? Will you collapse at the next rest stop, very much like this one, where a family of pine trees, very much like these, bends from the weight of the wind, paying homage to a god much kinder than ours?

Special

They say everyone deserves someone special, but I know people who don't, like the ones who didn't visit when I sat lame on my frigid front porch, reading Faulkner and sipping lypocene-laced green tea. But squirrels came with their empty stomachs, and telemarketers phoned in their hollow promises. Cars passed, too, with their steely glares, and that was something. I was shaking my cane at a stay-at-home mom from across the street. She was leaning on a baby jogger, taunting me. "You're lazy," she yelled. "You're giving me the creeps." I smiled, hoping a blood vessel might burst inside her head. "I ain't quittin' yet," I yelled, leveling my cane at her. At the time, I was trying to write something important, a hopeful book a stay-at-home mom might read, one a truck driver wouldn't throw out the window to make room for a fifteen-year-old runaway, who'd go down on him in Reno for a ride to L.A.

The New Tough-Guy Poet

The new tough-guy poet wears tight black T-shirts and lifts weights, writes about factories he's never worked in, drugs he's never taken. He pounds on tables, especially in bars. "What are you looking at, faggot?" he yells, just to shock people. Yeah, he's the new tough-guy poet. Girls go wet over his blue eyes and tattoos from Vietnam. They go wet when he's angry, when he's really pissed off. He's the new tough-guy poet. He's never been to Vietnam. He tells people he's part black. "I'll lay a nasty mojo on you," he shouts, then pounds on a table. Never knew his father, never knew his mother. His son hates him, his daughter hates him, his dog hates him. He's the new tough-guy poet, with shoulder-length red hair and a see-through eye patch. The Professors of Idiocy say his prose is "muscular," they say he's the "Next Big Thing." They pay him to get drunk. They pay him to get laid. They're happy because they're writing a book on him. They're happy because they want to be in this book. But the new tough-guy poet has flown off to the Millennium Poetry Party in Paris where he gets drunk with the old tough-guy poets. They pound on tables and swear in French. They puke on each other and swear in French. They punch out each other and swear in French. He doesn't know French. Even his English is pretty bad. But he's the new tough-guy poet, and he's offering you a new-tough-guy poem. He lays it in your lap like a live grenade. He lays it in your lap like a severed head.

Hurricane

They were watching a hurricane on TV, hoping someone would die, but just a weatherman with a receding hairline blown onto his ass. They were hoping someone would take a chance, suck on a downed power line or leap insanely off a pier wearing a circa 1558 life preserver, which is to say wearing nothing at all. In this poem the "they" is "you"—the uniformed hotel doorman, the short-order cook, the seamstress, the bulldozer operator making a terrible scene at the dentist's. Yes, it's you, whose better self gave up years ago, succumbing to stupidity and boredom. Hurricanes, tsunamis, massacres, droughts—this is how you live, waiting for death to nudge you with its big black horn.

"Hurricane"—from the Spanish *huracán*, from Taino *hurákan*; akin to Arawak *kulakani*, "thunder." Can you hear it?

Wordmeister

He dusts the shelves where his books used to be. He had some big ones—rock-hard abs, too—and he could half nelson a cliché until it screamed "mama." He was the Word's most wanted man, could steam into a library and shake up the joint. A rose broke into spasm when he read a poem about a rose breaking into spasm. There was a beautiful blonde in the front row with earrings fashioned from small No. 2 pencils; she had lapis lazuli eyes, her fingers bleeding from a thorn on a red rose she was womanhandling. He read a poem about wanting to be a woman in love with other women. He believed the phrase "flattened by a sacrament" could distract a terrorist, that the right word could bring the whole world down (or together), that he could let the stale air out of a century just by giving it a name. Poetry is Truth! Poetry is not Truth! Poetry can save the world! Poetry cannot save the world! All of this long before he had his teeth whitened and was given the Blowhard Emeritus Chair at the local college. Now just these empty bookshelves, a duster dangling limply from his hand, the image of a red rose quivering like a plucked guitar string in the hands of a beautiful and troubled woman.

Crazy Little Thing Called Love

I trapped the word called "love" and placed it in a museum where everyone set off alarms by coming too close. I knew a woman who could make her breasts bounce through positive thinking. Her name was Lois or Louise—a real lousy lay, according to a meathead poet. So I placed the plastic jar in Tennessee where only a few ants showed up. I gave a speech about The Five Kinds of Love but couldn't remember the fifth, so I broke the jar and donned my ragged Stetson, drifting toward a picture window lit by two glasses of red wine. And is that my wife in her red satin nightie? And oh, Sweet Thing, did I spell nightie right? Which makes her laugh. Tonight, nothing hateful to stain our canvas of love— just a little bad girl poetry with optional ice.

Love Story

We broke down in a little seaside town where soap made from whale sperm went for ten dollars a bar. The car mechanic bragged his TV had only three channels and that everyone's house smelled like meatloaf. While he fixed the car, we lunched on the beach, desperately needing to create a "moment" to remember when our yet-to-be-born children would hate us. I stroked her hair, told her the human brain was like a shower nozzle. She compared it to a skunk, but neither of us could explain the grounds of likeness. It was the Death-of-Metaphor Decade. You could say a car looked like a tropical fish and no one got it. Walking the beach, we discovered a worn leather glove and debated its history, then took a chilling tour of a local winery. When we paid the mechanic, he said that if every living chicken were lined up, they'd circle the earth eight times—a sad and troubling fact—but it was time to leave, the town disappearing behind us as if it never existed.

My Father Wasn't an Alcoholic

He didn't wet his pants at my First Communion or make drunken passes at my girlfriends. He didn't beat my mother or hide his bottle of Scotch in the baby's room. He never broke down and asked for forgiveness, never stumbled or puked in public. For years, he rode a crane and delivered mail. He never dropped a load of steel on anyone or stole welfare checks. He didn't teach me how to shave or swing a bat, never slobbered obscenities when I struck out. He wasn't even at the game. He was riding a crane, for Christ's sake; he was delivering the mail. I was my own masthead, my own backfield in motion. Can't blame him if my antlers got battered, my brain kebobed and curried. He never rolled me a fat one or brought Jack Daniel's to my lips, never cut my face out of the family photo album. He wasn't an alcoholic, he wasn't a mean man. In fact, he was rarely home.

Talkin' 'Bout My Generation

"The end of a poem should sound like the click when a box closes."
Whose box? Not mine. I don't even own a box that clicks. Just one of
the many lies we've been told, or tell each other—about this current
war, for instance, or that we'll live to be eighty without drooling all over
ourselves. What fools and liars—all of us at Woodstock, stoned on
drugs and sex, when in fact we were home cutting the front lawn or
enrolled in Kaplan courses; all of us protesting the war when in fact we
were stretched out on couches, hungover, watching reruns of *I Love Lucy*
while well-paid doctors swore we had twelve toes and four testicles.
And free love? Invented by men, for men. Even my father knew that.
We're the ones who won't say boo! to our children, who listen to rock
and roll sell SUVs, golf balls, tampons. And let's not forget my friend
who dropped acid with his son, crooning "Yellow Submarine" into a
camcorder—something meaningful to share while he's dying of prostate
cancer, saving up cash to freeze himself for the next century. How's that
for The Big Chill? How's that for t-t-t-t-talkin' 'bout my generation . . .

The Robert Bly Affair

(for R. E.)

It happened the year I began calling myself Tomaz and having lengthy public conversations with myself. I would say, "Tomaz, you shouldn't spend more for a good ukulele than a bad breakfast," things like that, things I thought Robert Bly would like. Of course, I didn't know Robert Bly, though he kept entering my dreams—once, maneuvering a flying motorcycle over a mountainous Frankenstein terrain; another time, opening and closing a car door for my wife at least a hundred times. She was naked and liking it. Or he'd leap from a cloud to play catch with my son or nurse the baby with his manly breasts. "O Silent One, O He Who Knows Nothing," he would scowl, as I practiced "Dueling Bashos" on my blues harmonica, or fondled the stone breasts of a snow woman he'd constructed. Awake, I wrote about octopi, miniature conifers, the rubbery wings of a bat. But, still, he entered my dreams, dissatisfied, chasing my wife around the backyard or measuring the shadow of a stick with my traitorous son. I wrote a poem called "The Banshi Pig Dance," which he said lacked "sacred space between words." I practiced walking like a penguin, but he said, "The memory of an insult hurts worse than the insult." I didn't know what that meant, but my wife and son did, curled around him like worms feasting on an apple—all this the year I began calling myself Tomaz, the year I began having lengthy public conversations with myself.

Couvade

I'm lying in bed, sipping a cup of pregnancy tea, my book obscured by a pillow under my shirt. Outside, the backyard's blanketed with a new breed of birds. And it's the middle of January. Take my teenage son, for instance—not only alienated, but indeed an alien, even wears a bandanna so we don't see his horns. According to my *What To Expect When You're Expecting Book*, "Enjoy Sex More Even If You're Doing It Less." "Let's decorate the baby's room," my wife says, "let's take hot showers." But my feet are swollen, my nipples sore, and I'm peeing like a racehorse. "Let's go skiing," she says. "Let's clean the garage." But my abdomen's itching, I'm constipated, and I've just opened to Chapter 21: "Preparing for the Next Baby." My wife's on the floor, doing one-arm pushups, smiling like a Buddha. "Bring it on," she says. "Bring it on!"

Mr. President

(for "W")

Somewhere, an intern buys underwear for the President. Probably on-line and with great agitation. I want to tell this President, "The self is a source of infinite possibilities." Convince him to spend time alone, prefe-rably in the air, tumbling thirty floors onto the hood of a black lim-ousine with absolutely no idea who pushed him; or maybe to imagine himself staggering across an Iraqi desert with shrapnel in his left thigh, or living with a prosthetic nose until he blows out his brains on a reality-TV show created just for him. Mr. President, please stop signing those stupid papers, stop listening to fat guys in blue suits who spend all day kissing the tops of gold fountain pens. And if you're counting on another life, don't think that old girlfriend will reappear on Mars in a century or two, giving you head in the backseat of your executive spaceship. My dead friend Neil would've known what to tell you. He was a philosopher who spoke in riddles, except when working on his house. He knew the name of every tool and could fix everything, except his fractured skull. He would've made us all lock hands and stupidly sing, "When our hearts go explaining, they go alone. Oh, lonely heart! Oh, lonely heart." That was a joke, Mr. President, a joke from a head saddened by bad dreams and temporal explosions. My head, your head.

Good Old Days

If I ever think of the "good old days," of conversations that shook me to the bone or made me run home to make love to my wife, those conversations won't be with poets, that's for sure. With priests either (except for one). There'll be no poets or priests in my pantheon, just a bunch of nobodies who made me laugh, like this old guy repeating, "Shit, damnit," amazed as my four-year-old reels in another fish. No, no poets or priests in my pantheon. No philosophers either, except for my dead friend Neil who said starfish can have as many as fifty arms. We were at the beach, waiting for a metaphor to wash up on shore, or a dead seal we could resuscitate. "Sometimes," Neil said, "you spend years tracing the roots of a tree only to find out it's a tree." "Most definitely," I replied, "like when I had my aura photographed in Las Vegas. It looked and vibrated like a jellyfish, yet I knew it was just an aura." He nodded, and we laughed, haply hip to the moment—the kind of laughter I'll never share with a poet or priest, the kind that branches out and trembles, lasting for weeks.

The Search for the Truth Continues

I believe in the life of the soul. I even believe in God. Thor, too, and I tremble every time his hammer thunders. I also believe Jesus is everywhere. This Christ is fat and dirty and snatches cigarette butts from the sidewalk. This other Jesus wears red stilettos and a dead animal around her neck. And then there's Atheist Jesus, who thinks having no answer is the answer, who wrote the "I Hate All Towelheads Polka," the "Kill All Faggots Hop." He works the counter at Cumberland Farms and has a toupee that looks like a tarantula . . . So many Jesuses, it's best to retire to my little cottage in Whatville where maple leaves hum a music only I can hear, and Japanese Zelkovas are just a stroll away. Where strawberries flourish in boot-sucking mud, and ants are preparing a pilgrimage—tiny white crosses on their backs.

Field Trip

"It's sure cold," the cemetery guard says, "but at least it's not snowing"—
conversation suggesting our lives are better than we think, when often
they aren't. Instead, the wind howling through pin oaks and sugar gum
trees that wear name tags and sway like drunken conventioneers stagger-
ing through the night. I point out a monument to my little boy, omitting
that a year ago a woman was raped and beaten to death as these same
trees looked on. It was hot that night, the gates locked, which accounted
for people's lack of sympathy. *What was she doing there, anyway?* Today
is a field trip of sorts. The microscope needs feeding: a dead leaf or pine
cone, maybe a disembodied claw. I like to think she had a fight with her
boyfriend, disappearing over a wall of rocks, wanting to shake him up.
It was just a "stupid thing" I want to tell my boy, thinking there should
be a special word for such a "stupid thing," a word that would resonate
through time, like the cry of a child falling from a thirty-story window.

Bad Behavior

When will the cops, asleep or gliding down asphalt pavements, get the call? When will children be taken away? . . . A little thing, an episode: many drinks, a few pills, a bit of playful grappling. Later, they made love when she was half-asleep, or maybe unconscious. He's not sure. This confession, over a mean cup of java in an understated coffee house, when we should be at the zoo, watching our children mimic a penguin's walk. "She's my ex-wife," he says. "We'll laugh about this later." He let himself go when he moved out, abandoning his Bowflex and West-Coast diet books. No more barbecues in the backyard where we'd all drink wine and watch four-year-old boys lunge at each other with Styrofoam swords. No more roasting marshmallows over a jerry-built brazier. I want to tell him I'm not the concierge, nor do I have the key to the secret garden. And I'm still waiting for the *Grammar of Marriage* book to arrive. And yes, she'll be angry, though mostly at herself, and every time I see her, I'll look away, or stare into my Palm pilot, which is really my palm, hoping for directions on how to behave, or how not to.

The New York School Poem

I had a favorite poet until he kept writing about his friends, Beau and Binkie, how they got drunk and tweezered hair from their noses, then thought they discovered a new way to make love, not realizing the Neanderthals had invented it. Yeah, I liked this poet until he described how Gloria got knocked up by Chrétien, who mainlined heroin into his temple while "Walk on the Wild Side" blared in the background, and how Chrétien survived, so Rashid wrote a song about it, which he'd chant at the end of Chrétien's readings. Boy, I would have liked this poet more if he hadn't felt obliged to write about Mahi's depression memorabilia, which he stole from scenes of real suicides, or about how Joanie, after a near-death experience, believed the best part of her had come back as a car alarm, or if he'd just been happy to be another Bukowski, a drunk who didn't care if anyone read his poems, and who despised his friends and ex-girlfriends even more than his friends and ex-girlfriends despised him.

The Worst Love Poem Ever Written

I come to you like a coyote with one leg, wound tighter than Paris Hilton's thong, while in the sky a hot air balloon hisses, *The language of love is the language of love.* And if I say, "Meet me at the golf simulator on deck 13," don't affect ignorance, though love is like that, and I, like a rubber-soled elephant trainer, weep to see the dinghy of your love disappear. Where? Behind that cloud, that wave. An argument would help, or a blind date with oneself. *Dave, stop. Stop, will you? Will you stop, Dave? I'm afraid.* That movie was great and always makes me think of you, which raises the question: "Who sunk the male boat?" Yes, I said that, in spite of the condom stuck to the floor like a deflated raft, in spite of our labial exercises, mostly arriving during sleep, like a posse of reporters awaiting a drive-by beheading. Bestir! my love-brain cools in the wine cellar of your tornadic frown. I'm talking about Valentine's Day when you gave me morning glories that overtook the house. You said you had a craving for glassware, for ebony canes, and flat screen TVs, while the frigid love birds sang all day in falsetto. In return, I gave you the square root of possibility and a verb which could save the world if I knew how to pronounce it—something like *drowsy* or *dorsal,* a word to replace the one called Love.

Love: an old man with a broken wrist, his white beard glimmering in the moonlight. Oh, yeah.

Happy

In spite of persistent rumors, let me assure you I'm happy. Happy as my well-fed pug and blue-eyed infant. Happy as the Brazilian beauty in a red thong cavorting half-naked on the Travel Channel. Happier than the local loony screaming at the same tree every morning, convinced it's an enemy from a past life. I'm happy I can say, "Don't go away I've got the baddest poem right here in my back pocket," and no one thinks I'm nuts. Happy for artificial putting greens, yellow buses that swallow up children yet no one gets hurt. Happy for tuna fish and the piano player at Nordstrom who asked me to sing along. Crusty sand dunes, orchids, a solitary grayish cloud frozen in the sky—I'm happy for them. Happy for the rust-colored bottom of a rap diva, for the ant-sized beauty mark on my wife's bum. Happy a fifty-five-year-old man can dance and play air guitar in his boxer shorts while his teenage son laughs himself silly. Even happy for Plan A, though I'll never understand it, and for the chance, no, pleasure, to spend a few idle moments inside this here ellipsis . . .

Y'all come back now

Continued from copyright page

Grateful acknowledgment is also made to the following anthologies which included some of these poems:

Poetry Calendar 2008 and 2007, both edited by Shafiq Naz (Alhambra Press); *Formes Poetiques Contemporaines*, Vol. 4 ("Prose"), edited by Michel Delville (Paris/Brussels: Les Impression Nouvelles, 2006); *The Smile at the Foot of the Ladder: A Prose Poem Anthology* (Obscure Publications, 2004); *Poetry Daily Anthology*, edited by Diane Boller, Don Selby and Chryss Yost (Sourcebooks, 2003); *The American Prose Poem from Poe to the Present*, edited by David Lehman (Scribner, 2003); *No One Out There Is Looking for Us: 24 Prose Poets*, edited by Ray Gonzalez (Tupelo Press, 2003); *Vespers: Religion & Spirituality in Contemporary American Poetry*, edited by Virgil Suarez and Ryan G. Van Cleave (U. of Iowa Press, 2003); *Like Thunder: Poets Respond to Violence in America*, edited by Suarez and Van Cleave (U. of Iowa Press, 2002); *American Diaspora: Poetry of Displacement*, edited by Suarez and Van Cleave (U. of Iowa Press, 2001); *Heartbeat of New England: An Anthology of Contemporary Nature Poetry*, edited by James Fowler (Tiger Moon Press, 2000); *Always the Beautiful Answer: A Prose Poem Primer*, edited by Ruth Moon Kempher (Kings Estate Press, 1999); *The Party Train: A Collection of North American Prose Poetry*, edited by Robert Alexander, Mark Vinz, and C.W. Truesdale (New Rivers Press, 1996).

I would also like to thank the National Endowment for the Arts, the Rhode Island State Council on the Arts, and The Academy of American Poets for fellowships and awards that greatly helped during the years these poems were written. Finally, a thanks to Dennis and Elaine at White Pine and to all my prose-poem buddies, who were there for me from the beginning.

Peter Johnson has published three books of prose poems: *Pretty Happy!*, 1997; *Miracles & Mortifications*, 2001; and *Eduardo & "I,"* 2006. He is also the author of a book of short stories, *I'm a Man* (White Pine Press, 2003), and two novels: *What Happened* (Front Street Books, 2007) and *Loserville* (Front Street Books, 2009). For his poetry, he has received a National Endowment for the Arts Fellowship, a Rhode Island Council on the Arts Fellowship, and his second book of poems was awarded the 2001 James Laughlin Award by the The Academy of American Poets. This award is given to honor a second book by an American author. His novel, *What Happened*, received the Paterson Prize for young adult fiction and was named the Rhode Island Book of the Year for secondary schools. He founded *The Prose Poem: An International Journal*, which he edited for nine years, and he is a contributing editor of *The American Poetry Review*, *Sentence*, and *Slope*. He lives in Providence, RI with his wife and two sons. More information on and interviews with Peter Johnson can be found at **http://www.providence.edu/English/Faculty/Peter+Johnson.htm.**